ELIZABETHAN

VII

JONATHAN LOVEJOY

Jonathan Lovejoy

ELIZABETHAN

The Complete Poems of
Elizabeth Peele

Volume VII

Jonathan Lovejoy

✝ Armageddon Publishing

Cover: *The Wave*, 1896
William Adolph Bouguereau (1825-1905)

ISBN-10: 0692319247
ISBN-13: 978-0692319246

For every Elizabeth

Introduction

Carmen Angelina Coletti (Elizabeth Peele) was perhaps the greatest composer who ever lived. After her death, studies of her music revealed a body of work—almost exclusively instrumental—of such beauty and power as to defy description. Even so, her lifelong reclusiveness rendered them obsolete to the world, and these musical treasures may remain apart from public view forever.

Even those few who heard her original scores did so in quiet apprehension, that this beautiful widow—lost somewhere deep in North Carolina farming country—brought forth music as completely ingenious as any ever written before. The sounds of greatness flowing from this woman's piano, surely this is not meant to be! For what purpose can she truly serve as a neoclassical composer in a jaded modern world, except as a curiosity and eventually, a fountain of eternal exploitation?

But while music did serve as a profession for her since she was twelve—her only wage being a sound mind and spirit—there was still another expression, both private and unintentional, equally meant for her eyes only. Gathered posthumously, so few of these "assemblies" can be called unique or special, and likely cannot set her apart from any other lonely poet in the world. But still they live on, as a glimpse into the mind of a musical genius and abused woman of Faith. Written parallel to her music over the years—with no striving for greatness or immortality—these poetic trifles, ironically, may be the only compositions of hers the world will ever hear.

Jonathan Lovejoy

ℰLIZABETHAN

or

"The Assemblies"

Volume VII

Jonathan Lovejoy

Such is the grandest music among us—

Poets…

Such are the wildest thoughts among us—

Composers…

The Book of Diana

195th Assembly

917

Daytime under a blackened sky

Winds begin to blow

Lightning shows the whirlwind

Twirling to and fro

918

*F*our cameras see the artists' pain

Unrequited need

On the eve of a new rain

Messages to heed

919

In the field of blizzard snow

Certainty is lost

'Til the white spider appears—marked yellow

To show the way home

920

Jumping over the canyon gorge

Waiting to fall in

Carried to safety by a miracle

To the other side

Jonathan Lovejoy

196th Assembly

921

Closets strewn with merchandise

Played in the minor key

Impossible to yield what I am searching for

In the House of Antiquity

922

Rossini wine tastes best to me

Beautiful—sublime to me

All others taint of inferiority

Save Mozart—whom I crave equally

Non-acoholic request is Best

When drinking among the rest

Partake of no wine—wherein is to excess

Forsake thy part of drunkeness

Life alone is access aplenty

To Sorrow and Regret

923

I have no greater pleasure

Than to stroll the garden

Looking for a treasure

Say "Beg thy Pardon"

To the Bee whose work I see

Though casually interfere

When I pick the brightest flower—

My gift—to measure

924

Where in the world would we be

Without looking glass psychology

That self-same absorption to the wire

From terror's thief be-twine

All hail! The chief of bricklayers

Choking in the dust

At the foot of the skyscraper—none too tough

In the house of falling debris

Jonathan Lovejoy

197th Assembly

925

Something strange is going on here

Like something is on his mind
Something fleeting—

But what?

926

The daguerreotype bears thine uncertainty

On the beaches of Normandy

In the sun, the sand, the wind, and the waves

And God's favor by the sea

927

Boys in the hood are up to no good

Shooting, killing, dying in the streets

In the arms of their creator—

Greets

After they have died—what then?

For the souls they left behind

And for the journey they must partake

From this earthly plane

Never a dull moment on the streets

For the boys in the hood

Where evaluations—of their safety are determined

By the mood other people are in

928

When the blackbird flies into the building

An explosion will occur

Beneath the tower of fallen dreams

Rests a new world of fertile green

Jonathan Lovejoy

198th Assembly

929

The biggest fish devours all others
Whether on land or sea
Be it the page or the big screen
Without apology

Growth is determined by Predestiny
A factor unforeseen
There is no manufactured prediction
Upon who will be Queen

Kings rule the court of Predestiny
Devouring all at will
Done without bloodshed if doable
Or flesh and bones to kill

The biggest fish devours all others
Whether at land or sea
King of the waters where predators rule
In Divine Predestiny

930

A final resting place, have I
Would that it were near
If there be no rest—
This side of living, then—
Bid thy servant "come"

The land before me is wilderness
None to call my own
Bless me permission
By grace—to beseech thy throne—
"I want to go home"

931

In preparation for my burial
Trouble times two awaits
Aflame upon the Coals of Death
Where expectations die

Along the road to nowhere
Fear is factored for some
While others con and steal their way
To the other side

Offspring rides foolishness to naught
Nothingness disguised in red
Akin to boats upon dry land
As useless as the dead

The condemned awake in grogginess
Child with nowhere to be
Stumbling in a darkened room
Without a life to see

Elizabethan VII

Five upon the world stage
By Destiny alone
Believing they are responsible for
What treasures that they own

In preparation for my burial
Trouble times two will wait
Until the angel comes to escort me home
Beyond the Golden Gate

932

Even though I had wished for Life
He did not wish for me—
From the beginning there has only been
An empty road to see

Life grinned a phony smile at me
Then beckoned me to ride—
Unbeknownst, I boarded his chariot
My soul I gave to pride

We drove beyond the Halls of Learning—
Expecting to know a way
Seeing other misdirected souls
Lost in their final day

In hope, I cruised the empty roads—
We passed the forest trees—
When I saw that they were skeletons
My heart raced ill at ease

Life assured that we travel on

Elizabethan VII

Until our pace was done
Behind the Forest of Dying Leaves—
I felt the setting sun

We detoured away the empty road—
Across a Field of Green
We rode along the Grassy Plain
To where I'd never been

I gazed with hope toward my driver
With unbelieving eyes—
When I learned he was not Life at all—
But Death in brief disguise

I grieved in fear for what I knew
Wishing for what I'd known
But he showed me the marker in the ground
A place to call my own

Jonathan Lovejoy

199th Assembly

933

Is there a melody in the clock—
The ticking of a clock?
Is there a rhythm in the heart—
The beating of a heart?

Time draws a harmony
From the music of the clock
It regulates a pace
By the rhythm of the heart

History is a concerto
Played in the flow of time
A rhythm from the steady heart
To melodies of the clock

934

Greatness will not show herself

To them who seek her hand

She hides her face from those who wish

To bind her with a band

Her company is Humility

The one she looks to know

When she finds out who is humble

To him will Greatness go!

935

A honeybee buzzed me back to life
When I thought that I had died
Death was only a daydream, then
A lovely place to hide

I woke up in the Garden Lawn
Beneath a flowering tree
Afternoon bade growth to roaming shadows
A summer's day had sung

936

Prayers I pray hath vanished away
In the cool of the evening day
As shadows draw nourishment from the twilight
Beneath the fall of Night

Storm clouds hath dispersed away
In the glow of a dying day
The first starlight reveals itself
In the glory of His throne

Amber clouds hath died away
In the blue of a grieving day

Jonathan Lovejoy

200th Assembly

Jonathan Lovejoy

937

Would that the bird were normal again

Feathers to the wind

Soaring the heights of his birthright

In lovely feathered wing

Content to ride the Winds of Memory

While others chirp and sing

The bird sits inside its cage

Undeterred—

Unburdened by the pain of knowing—

It will never fly again

938

Happiness is never known
To all but a blessed few
These picked a rose—but never a thorn
Hath pricked their finger red

For them—unhappiness is akin to
A coffin for a bed

939

I hear whispers in the waterfall

Saying "come hither"

Be they angels or demons—whether

This I do not know

940

Behind closed doors—a Christian family
Filled with lust and sin
Though not to be blamed the least bit for
The condition they are in

Sin is a disease which plagues us all
No need to come undone
Because God so loved the world
He gave His only begotten son

For without this sacrifice there would be—
No Christian family

201st Assembly

941

A helpless gaze into the sky
Certain, sudden death—
So cry!
Daytime has turned to night, oh my!
 Kiss your mother goodbye!

There's no life left to live
No one on Earth is prepared
For what the Night Cloud has to give
Look up—no lie
Death is coming by!

They call it the Night Cloud, you ask, why?
 Look what it did—
To the sunlit sky!

Jonathan Lovejoy

942

The Folly of Martha Corrine

A neglected grave is a shameful thing
A mountain voice—perturbed
Wistful moan—beneath the weeds
 Her coffin undisturbed

A neglected grave is a needful thing
The Messiah's voice is heard
Let the dead, bury the dead
 Rest memories undeterred

Have no tears for the dear departed
Rather alike in kind
Weep instead the souls accursed—
Of those they left behind

943

The lips of a strange woman taste bittersweet

A river of desires, running deep

Prevent thyself this forbidden treat

Though it be confined to the world of sleep

A ride with her is a pleasure trip

Lovely lust and sin

But a quick walk reveals her chariot to be

A poisoned spider's den

Jonathan Lovejoy

944

O dreadful serpent—thy wicked expression!
Gazes unto me
With nary a pinhead's worth of power
Given from above

Strike! This weary hand obliges
Poison from your ire
Then a shake—thou writhing carcass
Cooking in the fire

202nd Assembly

Jonathan Lovejoy

945

The blue pacifier brings ridicule

From the unworthy elite

On their superiority stroll

To the Great Theatre Hall

946

God's blessing may not come overnight
It may come over time
Languished upon the calender
The oath of His to chime

Beyond tomorrow, thy Word is known
Upon our sorrow, through mercy shown
His promises sublime

947

On a stroll through the empty Knowledge Hall
Known by another name
To dwell the wisdom of those who shun
World wide fortune and fame

Fearful rendezvous with the Lord
Whim of the knotted ivory chord
The unavoided game

948

*B*neath the deep blue sea

Where incongruities surmise

Upon what current of disaster do these

Impossibilities arise?

Sharks maul by undeserving measure

Waterlogged trunks—no buried treasure

Eschatological demise

949

Imprisoned by a new eccentricity

Aloft in "Zuider Zee"

Desires for the rhythm of it

But being unable

A craving for the rhyme of it

Enabled to transform

Somewhere near Eidelwiess and Brewer

Labeled as a "nothing

203rd Assembly

950

Pencils go "click" in the flow of night

Beyond unseeing eyes

What makes it go "tick"

The solemn relic Demonic in disguise

Flutes play on as they torment

To battle their discord

Angel guardians detect

The Lord doth protect

With mighty flaming sword

Unclaimed Spirits dispersed away

An unrelenting fright

Bassoon! A passion flame!

Flickering ghosts—all the same

Burned in the flow of night

951

Over familiarity is a mountain of labour

Causing babbling explanations—

To be necessary

952

Many acquaintances cannot be trusted

To paint the second mile

At any given moment—

Sensibilities will turn

Betrayal with a smile

953

When Opportunity knocks at 10 am

Where on Earth will you be?

At work, at play, asleep all day

Open the door and see!

Success will find you when you're ready

Someone was heard to say

If Opportunity goes ungreeted—at the door

Its knock will go away

Jonathan Lovejoy

204th Assembly

954

Tyrannosaurs stomp the land

In craving for a meal
Charcoal gray skin with crimson bands

In horrors to reveal

Though Revelation beasts are figurative

Their appetites are real

The Antichrist will stomp the Earth

Hungry for a meal

955

On my journey through the Valley Forest
Unbeknownst of where I've gone
The unknown rises all around me
Saying, go thy glory home

As I cruise along the River of Fate
Trees uplift in splendor
A guide to the Sea of Destiny
Saying, go thy glory home

Fearful trip through the Valley Forest
To a place I've never known
Grieving for the Voice of Heaven
Saying, go thy glory Home!

956

Fear crawls terror in my eye

Shaped and formed as a gun

Heroes brawl one to another

Until the war is done

Old problems do pass away

Does it matter how odd?

Every demon in Hell retreats

The awesome power of God

957

A mute murders a minister in Israel

Shot for the world to hear

With no rhyme or reason for his action

Although the Word is clear

This age is coming to an end

Shown from Antiquity

Evil waxes worse and worse

In Hell's iniquity

Satan's ubiquity is law

Eve of the piano train

Cast thy worries into the sea

Relish the Garden Rain

Jonathan Lovejoy

205th Assembly

958

The window opens at night

On winds of renewal—

I take a flight

Upon the breeze uncaring

Beneath the stars, as I please I ride—

I fly—above the trees

Fading forward in the moonlight

To live a life of ease

Is my fervent desire

Carrying me aloft

To the stars of the second heaven

High above—the feeble lights below

Man must obey

The curious sensation for flight

This, upon a journey along

The night breeze—in lieu of sleep

Where the voice of the Creator can be heard

Elizabethan VII

Saying, return hither—

And go—

Awake and feed my sheep!

959

Her draperies caress in amber
Across the sea of blue
Gray silhouettes, yon violet sheen
Faded into smoke

Drifting across her color scheme
Imparted by this light
Dipped below the evening line
Vanished into night

Sky at rest—beneath the day
Where summer's balmy rest
Uncovered by the vanquished ray
A sunlit turn to night

A watered vapor—gathered on
Indigo fades to gray
Above these sounds of approaching dark
Daytime banished away

960

Stand on your own two feet again

Like you have done before W

here incongruities meet again

At the apocalyptic shore

A blazing ride over the countryside

Backward with a mask on

Reveals the oath of stupidity

That some have pledged to live

Others give themselves to vanity

Money times seventy seven

Beauty and riches go hand in hand

On the catwalk of broken dreams

Others scheme in legal ease

Beauty and intellect to spare

 Assured of their place as superior

An arrogant blinder on

961

Superman plays the screen of our minds

A fire of red and blue

Carried aloft by the man of music

Through the universe—and beyond

Of this sort—there can report no other

Rules the court of like and kind

It won't be self destructive when you speak

When "JJ" holds down the fort

Aborted plans bring no tears

For those acquainted with this sport

Can I use your brain for a moment, Pam?

To see where it is I am?

962

Psalm 49 holds the key to life

Endeavor to break free

The ancestry sits bewildered

Under a cloud of "no"

Jessica knows how to escape

Ride with her to freedom

Crashing free of formal structure

Across the desert plain

Gaze toward the setting sun

Let conscious be your guide

As you speed toward the horizon

Trust in Him

Jonathan Lovejoy

206th Assembly

Jonathan Lovejoy

963

Break free of formal structure

Crash through her flimsy wall

Give her cause to regret thy notion

To answer another call

964

When confidence is gravely shaken

Then close your eyes and stare

Boldly to the Throne of Grace

Desperation for His embrace

Endeavor humility without disgrace

Make Providence aware

965

Is she prettier than me, the woman thought

  A frown turned upside down

This, at the counter in the mall

On the other side of town

She's prettier than me, the woman said

A smile turned upside down

This, in the parking lot at the mall

On the other side of town

966

Black limousines—

Pretty things

Campus of dreams

Murder schemes

They're gon' miss ya, son

On your train back to Georgia

You no good

You got no business 'round here no more

Flash! The college scene—

Campus of Lost Dreams Four sugar babies

In a poverty chariot

Braving the storm of hard labour

In beauty

In suppressed wealth

Repressed superiority

In the Omega Alpha Psi of it

Sorority of false hope

And lying dreams of innocence

Stroll the world!

Jonathan Lovejoy

Seek financial gain!
Ignore the pain of others—
 On your stumble to the top
 Your fumbling climb to the top
It doesn't matter who you kill— Does it?
Along the way
But duck your head—
When you hear the Whistle of the Boomerang—

Coming for you

207th Assembly

967

Shrubs need not be jealous of trees
Shadows beside the least of these
Darken the grass below

The wise weedling hath no cause to try
Climbing so far into the sky—

By way of calling and wayward girth
Trees have naught but rule the Earth
The seed grows their predestined form
As canopy thru every lightning storm

The shrub that embarks a climb so high
Will stretch itself too thin—and die

968

To glide the court of dreams

No help with which to lean

As a slide upon an icy pond—

No friction in between

Twilight all around me

No harm or fear to glean

An unimpeded path to right

The wrong my life has been

969

No babe, don't lie

Fergie's the reason why

Pick these peas—

No garden weeds—

One rose—

A thorny bouquet

970

Strolling the Isle of Merchandise

On the eve of monetary gain

The ancestry looks in bewilderment

Of the cometary power drain

In the face of the tormented one

They see a new inheritance

Threatening to lash them a hundred fold

With the whipchord of Heaven's vengeance

Don't look so bewildered, you two!

It'll only be what you deserve!

When the boomerang arcs around again

With your flesh against the curve

Cast thine wondering eyes away

No need to stare and wonder

Vengeance is mine, saith the Lord

And your bodies ripped asunder

Jonathan Lovejoy

The ancestry turns and looks away
In grief for what they've done
Tending the Isle of Merchandise
In fear of the tortured one

208th Assembly

971

The end of the yellow brick road is Death

Where the body lies

Despite what riches there may be

A closing of the eyes

Follow the yellow brick road of truth

To see where it may lead

The color of the cemetery grass and leaves

Is emerald, indeed

972

The road to freedom is blocked for me

The skeleton masses are too blind to see

Sabotaging deliberately

My trip upon this road

973

My coffin, my tomb

My grave—

My womb

974

*S*ome learn the truth when its too late

In the idyllic setting

A stroll among the forest trees

And the life they should have lived

A return to the city is their calling

Thirst for capital gain

Don't wail for it now, mister

Buck up and endure the pain

Jonathan Lovejoy

209th Assembly

975

Jonathan Lovejoy

In the Palace of the Golden Feast
Sits a man among the least of us
Engaging upon the beast within
Shopping his wares to get in

Loved ones brave the desperate call
Outside the door of tortured sleep
Remove the covering from thy mouth—
Endeavor a simple and chosen peep!

The ancestry babbles irrevalence
Where speech had eluded them
Backwards in the flow of time
Before their faculties had formed

Subcutaneous death ensues
In the lives of those who dare
To put their hands on the righteous child
For as much as even a scare

976

Sing praises to the most high

In spite of broken dreams

When filth corrupts the path to joy

By monumental means

Man deviseth a way to happiness

Through a feeble design

But there is no joy this side of heaven

Except by the Divine

Joy and sorrow are Predestiny

By birth for one to own

But the prayer of the righteous availeth much

Go boldly before the Throne!

977

One may see the form of God

Jonathan Lovejoy

Though not the fulness thereof
He spent the entire year on his back
 In a mental institution—

Two women dressed in black
Fight it out under the stars
Pulling, clawing one another's hair
While the angels look on

One can see the form of God
Though not the fulness thereof
Life and limb are barriers to Him
The preacher's robe, the Brothers Grimm

Slim chance of knowing
Condemned is more the game
Glimpse the Light when you can
You'll never see it again

978

Elizabethan VII

Sing his praises—Heaven is fine!

Heaven is fine!

Send praises to the highest mountain

Touch the clouds with thy finger!

Wait for mine entry—

Wait for mine entry!

Death may not stop me

Send in my father

Don—my will died

Tool it, my ride

Send in thy bride!

Qual o

Qual-o

See it thru

Do it in stride—

Qual-do it on the side!

Sing his praises—

Heaven is fine!

Heaven is fine!

Send praises to the highest mountain

Touch the clouds with thy finger!

Jonathan Lovejoy

210th Assembly

979

*D*on Giovanni was desperation

Born in a minor key

La Cenerentola was consolation

Most indisputably

Phrases from 1787

Farewell to tragedy

Interposed to 1817

Farewell to comedy

Heroes and heroines galore

The operatic stage

Songs through time and history

To end the earthen age

980

I pray that only good things will happen

Good things from here on in

Oh Lord, send blessings to my door

Banish away my sin

981

What you don't want is what you need

Regarding what you own

In the warehouse of cleaning wheels

Escape is never won

Strolling through the Halls of Labour

Looking for a reprieve

Finding no way through to freedom

And no pain to alleve

In the endless sea of labour

A Truth it pains to grieve
To find no rest for a weary heart
With new days to bereave

982

On the search for earthly solitude
There's no where left to go
Save the Alaskan wilderness—in—
A hundred miles of snow

On the search for Earthen solitude
I came upon a house
On a highway far outside of town
 An isolated house

Surrounded by naught but two neighbors
A hollering voice away
Separated by the road
That few were traveling on

Elizabethan VII

No sooner than I resigned among
This earthen paradise
Neighbors emerged across the road
Two nosier than mice

An eighty year old poverty ma
From great depression days
Yapping away on a cell phone
Inviting me a gaze

In the manner of her nosy way
She asked where I had been
Inquiring if I was a doctor
Then on her phone again

From around the back of this neighbor's house
Emerged another one
A man 35 years old at least
Most likely not her son

From the height of the Himalayas
To down Death Valley's floor
My paradise sank to nothing
Of what I'm searching for

Her gray house suddenly seemed a nest
Of congregated bees

Jonathan Lovejoy

Buzzing the hornet's ferocity
To kill my dream of ease

On the search for earthen solitude
There's nowhere left to go
Except the Alaskan Wilderness—in—
A hundred miles of snow

Elizabethan VII

211th Assembly

983

Disillusioned and world weary

With nothing but a pen

Ink from inside a reservoir

Too deep for hiding in

Lamentation—to no one

A calling—to abide

A depth of suffering—to the paper

My privilege—to provide

Jonathan Lovejoy

984

He said it when he left the Earth

To all children "be good"

Words of the extraterrestrial

His wisdom—understood

985

Spirits display upon the gridiron

Too dead to live

A perfect pass thrown

A life to give

Martyred for thug life

Took up the sword

Killed in the earthen prime

A perished sword

Risen up from poverty

To greatness born

Wishing to change the world

A life forlorn

Learning lessons too late

His soul to save

Jonathan Lovejoy

Gangster icon for eternity

An early grave

986

I long to go where Beauty lives

Somewhere apart from me

Above the highest mountain

Across the bluest sea

Behind this earthen fantasy

Awaits reality

Home is Heaven where Beauty lives

The place I'd rather be

Elizabethan VII

212th Assembly

987

Afraid to live—afraid to die
No explanation why
A stroll among the markers—where—

No expectations lie

988

My view—an unkept shrubbery
Mocking me—a weed
Grew too tall for itself—dying
Trying to be a tree

Both in the shadow of grandeur
Towering their grief
Residence of the honeybee—
Flowering their leaf

Elizabethan VII

989

The ice made itself known
In its water—cracked!
A piece of itself across the room
Mission to be heard

Fission occurred—a great noise
Tinkling by its peers
The last gasp before dying
Symphony of years

990

*H*ere is a song for Oedipus

Those who love peace, take wing

About a boy who murdered his father

Oh, what a dreadful thing!

The boy had spoke out of turn again

Suddenly afraid

When he heard his father's footsteps

The thumping sound they made

The boy swallowed a lump of fear

His sister left the room

When the footsteps appeared at six feet tall

Elizabethan VII

Screaming a voice of doom

Daddy, don't hit me anymore
The boy said with a tear
But the father started to take off his belt
Grabbing him by the ear

The belt lit fire into his body
Pain hit him like a flood
The belt bit pieces out of his soul
Cutting his skin to blood

The boy sat trembling when it was done
A whisper in his breath
The very next time he touches me
I'm going to beat him to death

Here is a song for Oedipus
Those who love peace, take wing!

Broken through the dawn and sunset
Of each and every day
The boy kept this promise to himself
To make his father pay

Late one rainy afternoon
The boy came home from school

Jonathan Lovejoy

Stressing out from a bad day
He broke his father's rule

When he saw his father's rage again
He whispered to himself
Then he grabbed the belt from his father's hand
And pushed him against a shelf

While the father stumbled backward
The son went raving mad
He struck his old man with a bat
With all the strength he had

The boy stepped over to his father
And hit him on the head
He did it over and over again
'Til his old man was dead!

When the cops answered the mother's call
They couldn't believe their eyes
They drew their guns when they saw the boy
But much to their surprise

The boy sat calmly in a bloody shirt
He hardly moved at all
A TV lay smashed on the dead man's head
A belt lay in the hall

Elizabethan VII

I told him not to touch me
He said under his breath
I told him if he touched me again
That I would beat him to death

While the boy did his time in prison
To God his heart he gave
After they released him on parole
He went to his father's grave

The son allowed himself to cry
With every tear he had
For the life he spent without a father
 For what happened to his dad

The man found love and marriage
In time they had a son
He fathered the boy in love and peace
Until his days were done

Here is a song for Oedipus
Those who love peace, take wing!
About a boy who lost his father
Oh, what a dreadful thing

213th Assembly

991

I will sing to her the love of bluebirds
On our golden stroll through every key
A song from the future drifts above her
To turn me into what I long to be

Jingle Bells do sing among the carols
Trees are heard so loud and clear
A snowfall above brightens our landing
To embrace the earth in joy this very year

Now the bluebird sings of love again
Long after the snow has gone away
Melodies are heard beyond the city
On a stroll where happiness may rule the day

992

A phonecall from another realm

Where trouble has begun

Cries of help from a boy to his mother

A plea from her only son

993

Naked—the woman ran down the stairs

To shock her husband unawares

Fear on her pretty face

A feeble heart—frozen still

Devils on the windowsill

Our Sunday hiding place

994

She said, "tell all the truth but tell it slant"

Beg them not to listen

Itching ears toward idolatry

Lying eyes to glisten

My guide beneath the Flowering Tree

Her message in the art

A lamp gathered from among them

Glows brightest when apart

Elizabethan VII

214th Assembly

995

*I*n the deepest part of the forest
Where the dead go to live
I was shown the remnants of a fire
With no power left to give

In frustration I endeavored to go
 To leave my host behind
He slumped over in disappointment
As though I'd been unkind

We left the Cemetery Forest
To see a movie show
Remnants of the dead were playing
With no more life to know

While I lie still beneath the grass
Roses above my bed
I see seven in summer bloom

Diaries of the dead

296

There is a conduit between Earth and Heaven

Unseen by man

Unknown to living eyes

Those who have died enter this

To begin their journey upward

Observing the last of the world through blue windows

Of the conduit

The ride goes quickly through the blue

Past the first heaven—

Into the blackness of the second heaven

Quickly through the universe

Past every glowing star

The end of the journey is the Throne of God—

In the third heaven

Those who look a mile above

Elizabethan VII

To see the blue tunnel rise

From the ground to the bottom of the sky—

Have died

297

Lost on a train to nowhere

Engaged along the way

In a conversation with the unwise

For what he had to say

We came upon a forest road

A ways outside of town

There resided a man of knowledge

Of no special renown

Disembark the train to nowhere

The road will lead you home

To prevent the coagulation of life

And tragedies unknown

998

In the castle I hear footsteps

Thumping down the hall

Terrifying me to no end

For no reason at all

Inspiration is fleeting

So grab it while you can

Or else it will abandon you

Like waves upon the sand

Never allowing me to rest

This demon with a verve

Taking every chance, around the clock

To vex my fragile nerve

Elizabethan VII

Jonathan Lovejoy

215th Assembly

999

*I*ve learned to live past December days

My heart to be broken a thousand ways

But I care about the future

No way that I won't choose her

No fair that I might loose her

In this December haze

There has to be a sign

That you forever will be mine

That you and me are fine

As no ordinary wine

You and me can never be apart

A thousand years with nowhere left to start

Let's say it to each other

There will never be another

That only you live inside my heart

Though the rain has stormed our lives again

Our love is remade anew

    Whether winter skies are ever blue

The only thing to know is true—

The one thing I know is forever true

I love you

1000

*H*usband—let not division have thy triangle!
Do not let desire rule the day
Curse the lips of a strange woman
Send them packing along their way!

It is the breaker of all deals
The anti-peacemaker that kills
To send a ripple through the fabrick of stability
To make it unstable

The walls become instability
Filled with cracks and fissures
This rumbling shall not cease
Until the walls of protection are down

And now, there is no protection
From the boomerang that was thrown

1001

Send Gretta packing along her way
Her creamy skin
Her rosy lips
Let not desire rule the day!

She enticeth by her lips
Alluring with her eyes
Come to my lonely room, dear Sir
A big surprise awaits

Her mouth is a chasm
A vortex of sorest need
Do likewise as Joseph hath done
And leave her to her greed!

1002

*W*isdom is the other side of sleep

On the awakening

Scattered about in the field of stones

Which clearly can be seen

Arise to gather them with haste

Lest they begin to fade

Stones of silver, gold and diamond

And emeralds of jade

216th Assembly

1003

Across the ocean to the sun

Before the evening day

To catch a glimpse of Glory Home

That vanisheth away

Beneath the clouds—this canvas

In burnished amber light

The pinnacle of earthen desire

Fading into night

1004

She doesn't know what to look for
In a man who murdered her husband
From the mist, he drifts into plain sight
Ready to be wed

Because of her new bridegroom
Her old husband was dead
His heart could not endure the strain
When he heard what she said

1005

Cruising the highway to nowhere
On fire with a plan
Learning that those around me
Have gone as far as they can

A new level of intolerance
Is written on their face
Desiring to be anywhere
Except this hiding place

Cruising the road to nowhere
Cool of the morning dew
Hope lies beyond the horizon
The place I'm going to

1006

Sin is fruit—

Touch it anew

Am I gone?

Sin is on!

Elizabethan VII

217th Assembly

1007

Symbols of my death still beckon

Calling me

To pull me from the flight to peace

Appallingly

Dying echoes the cave of spite

Enthralling me

A monster in the Ruins of Athens

For all to see

Jonathan Lovejoy

1008

We killed our mother dearly
 And buried her in the snow
 Our footsteps trailed from her grave to home
 With nowhere left to go

The violent years bore us in two
Berating us with what to do
Until we killed our mother dearly
And buried her in the snow

One night while she lay sleeping
We crept up to her bed
There bade an end to days of weeping
We smothered her 'til dead

We smothered her 'til breathing stopped
We drug her out of bed
We dragged her body into the cold

Elizabethan VII

Toward the winter wood

Sister and me in tow—adrift
In the wake of what we could
In the twilight snow we calmly stood
Toward the winter wood

Knowing what we had to do
Though not of what we should
We drug her body to the edge
Of the winter forest wood

Down through the winter white we dug
Into the hardened ground
We chopped into the frozen soil
Where our final strength was found—

We laid her in the dirt
Her grave raised into a mound—
We cleared away a foot of snow
And laid her in the ground

We smoothed the rounded dirt away
Where no marker would be found

The violent years bore us in two
With nowhere left to go
We killed our mother dearly
And buried her in the snow

Jonathan Lovejoy

Sister and me—we followed the trail
Of footsteps to our home
Looking each other in the eye
No remorse for what we'd done

Gazing beyond the clouds of winter
 To remember the fallen one
To hear the wind carry what we'd done
Beneath the setting sun

No tears were left for us to cry
Nowhere was left to go
When we killed our mother dearly
 And buried her in the snow

Now a voice cries in the wilderness
Winter winds begin to blow
Her children killed her dearly
And buried her in the snow

1009

The most subtil creature in the field

A slithering impression

Without compromise to yield

A most unholy expression

In colors beautiful to behold

A hiss and rattle to listen

The Puff Adder, the Gaboon Viper

Unearthly fears to glisten

Venomous beyond poison

Their sight, a quickening breath

A bite more poisonous than agony

A scalding, acid death

218th Assembly

1010

Slithering blue among the leaves

So goes the Ahna Din

This serpent needs no camouflage

Nor place for hiding in

Unique among every other

Shedding blue patterned skin

Or red, or yellow, or greenish hue

Whatever mood they're in

Jonathan Lovejoy

Never seen by human eyes
Except for now and then
Those who see it scream and die
Bit by the Ahna Din

1011

Talent without inspiration is mediocrity

In manufactured prose

The heart knows better than the mind

Of Hypocricy's repose

1012

They say that they can't slam it shut

For generations they've tried

The poverty door is open

To close it—they're unable

Money comes into their hands

Brightened by the day

The wind blows through the open door

Until their hopes are gone

In the rain of spring and autumn

Summer heat and winter cold

Jonathan Lovejoy

The poverty door is open—
To close it—they're unable

1013

In the morning I chopped a tree
To fashion myself a cross for me
A burnished cross—wooded pine
To mark this lonely grave of mine

The remaining wood—my fallen tree
Will make a lovely coffin
I could have ordered a marble stone
A fancy casket of my own

Elizabethan VII

I could have ordered a cushioned bed
But why—
When all I am is dead?

219th Assembly

1014

*I*vory sweetness half consumed

Where choices loom

Thy iron cage above ground

My grave and tomb

Ladybirds in amber feather

Jonathan Lovejoy

Imprisoned here
Beauty ensared by Destiny
Wisdom to hear

Birds twittered by evil
In tit for tat
Embittered capabilities
Of where its at

Iconic heroes masquerade
The road to Hell
Paved with good intentions
Christ rose to tell

1015

Alas! Alas! Another day!
Oh, sorest regret—
Another day!

Elizabethan VII

Children ride—horses play

Specific torture
Burning brain
A hole in the soul
Is all the same!

Alas! Alas! Another day! Sunrise—
Sunset— Another day!

Sorest regret—
Another day!

1016

Strangers in my hiding place
Souls I know—forgotten
While I lay hidden in terror
Wishing to God they were not in

Relatives that I once knew

Empty greetings galore
Years of kindness laced in venom
The Atramental Shore

Would that my sweat were gasoline
My breath, a flaming fire
I would display the meaning of a hug
Vengeance that I require

1017

Asleep—upon the awakening
Shades of clarity—in the fog
Though shadows—still—lurk
From the light of the Red Sun

Elizabethan VII

220th Assembly

1018

'Hardworking' is not a character trait

Unfit to be admired
'Kind' and 'Humble' are character traits

Greatly to be desired

There is dignity in all labour

Though no inherent good

Your Humility will be rewarded

By the hand of God

1019

Walk the grounds of the mansion home
Gray in the realm of the garden gnome
Medication on the lawn

Hear the soul of the widow scream
Her children on the money scheme
Before the break of dawn

A mother soon to kill and bury

Elizabethan VII

At the Mountain Pineview Cemetery

With mourners looking on

1020

Endeavoring to pick up a hop frog

As though I didn't care

But when I reached down to capture him

A song played in the air!

Melodies all around me

Risen up from nowhere

I looked and saw my little frog

No longer sitting there

My visitor had hopped away

From this melodic scare

Hiding in a place unknown

From prying eyes to stare

1021

*W*isteria Lane is a waterfall

Of modern desperation

From Ocean West to the Eastern Sea

Imprisoning a nation

Flowers in the Garden of Thistles

Grown tall among the weeds

Gathered to a thorny bouquet

Of unrequited needs

Lessons on immorality

Comeuppances galore

A mirror to the goings on

Behind the neighbor's door

221st Assembly

1022

$\mathcal{A}$short absence quickens love

A long absence kills it

Trust—

Is the mother of deceit

1023

The kids are going to eat me, the mother said

Waking up in a sweat

Nightmares of being cooked alive

 And served with vinaigrette

The mother rose from her grieving bed

 Into the mountain sun

Remembering every daughter of hers

She buried one by one

A strolling to their graves

A cooling of the day

By the whispering of the leaves

Drying her tears away

1024

Death comes in fine linen
To breathe solace to the child
Take no thought for her, dear sir
Her passing will be mild

Displaced by no hurricane
You're likely to forget
That this girl was taken by poverty
And ashen gray regret

Shed no tears for her passing
Her glory is to roam
From here to the gates of heaven

Elizabethan VII

Country road, take her home!

1025

*I*vory pillars—
At the gate beneath the shade
Made to guard the way to life divine
In our home beneath the Pine

A garden stroll
Underneath the Tree of Ease
These hearts toll adrift this evening time Of our
forest leaf sublime

222nd Assembly

1026

To even the angels, I have no beauty
Imprisoned monster troll
Desiring the company of others
But being unable

Good times may or may not happen
Determined by the mood
Riches are perceived as beneficial
And loveliness as good

Upon the Lawn of Rejection
Still hoping for a life
Understanding that there is none
When good times have come and gone

1027

Oh, precious Lord
There is no rest from crying
Sighing relief from your mighty sword
For where thy mercy is stored

Righteous Heaven
There is no hope to be found
Surround me with thine angels seven
My grieving heart to leaven

1028

On our stroll among the prairie green

Sights of beauty never seen

Farewell, unseeing eye

You need to leave them behind, he said

The former life you lived is dead

Look to this azure sky!

Sing the blessed breath, a hymn

Ergo the Star of Bethlehem

Redemption draweth nigh

Stroll the grounds of the prairie field

To gaze upon thy harvest yield

These blessings to rely!

Stroll the line of forest trees

To tend or repose as you please

The sea of prairie green

Take rest beyond the Harvest Feast

A mansion to the prairie east

The Home I've never seen!

1029

I heard my name called when
I died It was a somber tone
Prompting me to awaken
To see where I had gone

No stroking of the weary brain
No mourners all around
No owner to the disembodied voice
That made the husky sound

Upon the hearing I did awaken
Arising from my bed
Not hearing the voice again at all
That called when I was dead

223rd Assembly

Jonathan Lovejoy

1030

The storm of the beastly six of mine

Blows intrepidly in the wind

Worn out from days of grieving

Coming to an end

Oak burnishes the dining table

Stoked in a fetter's train

Lost on a boatline seaman

Ardent fever pain

In the house of the newness bird

I heard the favor sing

Crafted by melodies from above

 A cook-fried onion ring!

Stings too much to be eaten

Pays too much to give

Elizabethan VII

While the crimson flow is raining down
Shut up and let me live!

1031

Martha—a single leaf

Carried by the breeze
Above and beyond these prison bars
Away—thy life of ease!

Money will do you no good here
Inmates will spoil the mood
Captured by conspiracy
A more dour neighborhood

Cut down from the ivory tower
In prison walls alone
Devastated by winds of destiny
A greedy heart of stone

Stores of money and power
Ocean ships to roam
Wrecked on the shores of humility

Jonathan Lovejoy

A prison for a home

1032

At the party—in a photograph from 1934
I saw the face of antiquity gazing at me from before
The ghostly face of antiquity was burning at me from before
 My grandmother—and nothing more!

At the party—as a guest of Perpetuity and Lore
I gazed upon the faces of all those who had come before
Gazing upon the faces of all those who had come before
They were dead—and nothing more!

I looked heartily upon the photograph from 1934
Adrift among the forgotten dead as we danced across the floor
Adrift among the honored dead as we danced across the floor
A cemetery—and nothing more!

1033

Eyes of crystal—azure blue

Shimmered as the morning dew

In fear to look upon

Hair of midnight raven pitch

Lips of ruby to bewitch

So dear to look upon

224th Assembly

1034

I am weary of the dead land

And what it has to show

I wish to join the land of the living

The pain of life to know

I took her to the doctor

For what it was she had

It took her to the dead land

One hundred miles to go

1035

Conveying the Rule of Casper

To the train among the living
Fear distasteful as evergreen

Eleven seconds left to breathe

1036

Harry Potter nd the Kingdom of Heaven

Magic I will never know
Greatness 'stowed upon the Lady

A chamber of secrets below

Ghosts move about the castle

Clues whisper from the wren

Voices speak the order of the phoenix

The place I was hiding in

Burning in the goblet of fire

The half blood prince stood still

Make haste to find the sorcerer's stone

And the prisoner of azkaban to kill

This wouldn't have happened to me

If the nightfalls had been more white—

Chasing the boy wizard though the shadows

In the fall of night

A light to help guide the children

Jonathan Lovejoy

On their ride 'twixt wrong and right

1037

Lift thy head from thy shoulders

To see what is brewing on

All that is left of thee is death

And burial beneath the lawn

1038

Do you go through this with every author

What you went through with me?
Learning if it happens at all

It takes an eternity?

225th Assembly

1039

A face! A face!

Where none should be

Smiling, mocking

Laughing at me

Through the looking glass

I see Demonic banality

Eyes and a mouth—

Laughing at me

1040

Although he was a friendly sort

He had no sex appeal
Born without what ladies require

In their succulent meal

Watching others around him

Impress from head to shoe

Leaving him to his ugliness

And better things to do

1041

$\mathcal{I}$ found out they both hate me today

Mom said I finally got what I deserved

On the way to the hospital—

1042

*I*n every life, there is a day of reckoning

A time when purpose is revealed
  When the sum of days and years is tallied

  But along the way, many false reckonings will appear

  Having every bit the persuasive power of reason

  Leaving a person wrongly convinced—

  Of what their future may hold

226th Assembly

1043

They're not going to let me out anymore

The door is locked all the time now
I get so afraid at night—

1044

I remember my 1st whipping as plain as day

Mom was stadningin the doorway
I wanted her to help me—

1045

Days of failure as a person

Incredibly
Days above ground do worsen

Inevitably

If the righteous shall scarcely be saved

In the coming year

Then where, O Lord, shall the wicked

And ungodly appear?

1046

In front of the face of the Angel

In a North Carolina corner of the woods
If there's a hedge—

Tell them to step through the hedge

And clear a path for me

I'm not a cheerleader, she said—

Who told you not to listen?

Car trouble is car trouble

When your life is stopped on a dime

Don't do the crime, the trees said

And not expect to do the time

I would like to go with you—

But I cannot

Its time for me to get up

And see what life has got

I would like to see what's over the corner

Where the butterflies alight

This—let me tell you about it

Tim LaHay is Tim LaWho?

Jonathan Lovejoy

When it comes

In front of the face of the angel—

In a North Carolina corner of the woods

227th Assembly

1047

I was thirteen the first time I saw it

The first time I saw the lifeline

1048

In the evening time—the sunset

Where he was going to

The Grieving One was locked away

For something he didn't do

With a scream to end all screams

She proclaimed it to the wind

Though she was not a prisoner

For something she didn't do

On the shores of antiquity

Humble from head to shoe

Helping any way he could

His plans were done in two

When he fell in the spell of lock and key

For something he didn't do

But fate has a way of going through

With what it wants to do

So he was locked away for many years

Jonathan Lovejoy

For something he didn't do
No matter that he was innocent
His comeuppance was overdue

ABOUT THE AUTHOR

Jonathan Lovejoy is a graduate of the University of North Carolina at Greensboro, with a B.A. in Religious Studies. He currently lives in Winston Salem, North Carolina.

For more info on the author's life and career, visit jonathanlovejoy.com.

www.ingramcontent.com/pod-product-compliance
Lightning Source LLC
Chambersburg PA
CBHW060921040426
42445CB00011B/734